De Havilland

KEY
Books

HISTORIC COMMERCIAL AIRCRAFT SERIES, VOLUME 6

Contents page: The ill-fated G-ALYP seen on a test flight before delivery to BOAC. G-ALYP crashed into the sea off Elba on 10 January 1954.

Published by Key Books
An imprint of Key Publishing Ltd
PO Box 100
Stamford
Lincs PE19 1XQ

www.keypublishing.com

Original edition published by *Aeroplane* magazine as *The Comet* © 2012, edited by François Prins

This edition © Key Publishing, 2022

All images © Key Archive unless otherwise stated.

ISBN 978 1 80282 378 3

Typeset by SJmagic DESIGN SERVICES, India.

Contents

Introduction

By the end of 1942, Britain had been at war for over three years. It had been three very difficult years, and victory was far from assured. However, strategic bombing missions against enemy territory and success in the Middle East indicated that the tide was slowly changing. Assisted by the United States, which had by then entered the war, Britain was able to share the burden. However, defeat of the Axis powers could not be taken for granted, and in this climate, the War Cabinet sanctioned the formation of a committee to consider a post-war world of air transport. Appointed to chair the group, which included politicians, engineers, businessmen and aircraft builders, was John Theodore Cuthbert Moore-Brabazon (later Lord Brabazon of Tara). He was an inspired choice, as he was the first man in Britain to hold a private pilot's licence, and he had advocated and promoted aviation in Britain from the earliest days.

The Brabazon Committee also had the foresight to embrace an emerging method of propulsion: gas-turbine or jet engine technology. It, rightly, placed piston-engines – which were quite advanced at the time – at the forefront but also made a case for the gas-turbine. This enabled Geoffrey de Havilland and Ronald Bishop to begin building a pure-jet airliner to be powered by engines designed by Frank Halford. It was a very brave move from de Havilland, and one that gave Britain the lead over the rest of the world.

The de Havilland DH106 Comet aircraft made history as the first jet airliner to fly and also as the first to offer a scheduled jet passenger service. Even though more than 60 years have elapsed since that first flight, the story of the Comet continues to excite and inspire.

Chapter 1

De Havilland Comet

Through sheer necessity, many technological advances were made across the board during World War Two. One such advance was with the gas turbine or jet engine. While this method of propulsion had also been developed simultaneously by Italy and Germany, it was Frank Whittle's design that would prove to be the most efficient. Although Whittle had been dismissed as a crank by many, there were some who thought his engine had potential. Government funds to develop a prototype were slim, and it fell to others, such as Ernest Hives of Rolls-Royce and Frank Spriggs and Thomas Sopwith of Hawker Siddeley, to encourage and help. In 1941, the small experimental Gloster E28/39 aircraft – powered by a Whittle jet engine – flew for the first time and gave Britain a lead in gas-turbine technology.

First flying in September 1943, the de Havilland DH100 Vampire entered service with the RAF in 1946.

The de Havilland DH108 was built in 1948, in order to research high-speed flight, and it set a speed record of over 600mph.

On 7 December 1941, the United States was drawn into World War Two and immediately put its industrial might into action. The US had already been providing fighting equipment for Britain, but now it could really make progress. All types of ships, land vehicles and aircraft poured in from US manufacturers, which were developing concepts at a great rate. By 1942, the US had reached an agreement with Britain to provide transport aircraft, leaving the UK to concentrate on fighters and bombers. The ease with which the US could build transport aircraft had not escaped the British government, and it realised that by the time the war ended – and had been won – the US would simply convert their transport aircraft, such as the piston-engined Lockheed L049 Constellation

BEA Comet 4B at London Heathrow Airport. Scale supplied by a mechanic working in the nosewheel bay.

To test the engines destined for the Comet, Avro Lancastrian IV (VM703) was converted to carry two de Havilland-Halford Ghost engines in place of the outboard Rolls-Royce Merlins. Test flying commenced on 24 July 1947.

and Douglas DC-4, into airliners and take over the civil market that Britain had made its own in the pre-war years. Something had to be done. Thus, on 23 December 1942, the British government set up a committee to consider the requirements of the post-war airliner market and what types would be needed.

Under the chairmanship of Moore-Brabazon, the committee was made up of representatives from the Air Ministry, the Ministry of Production and the Ministry of Aircraft Production (MAP). Later meetings were attended by selected representatives from the British Overseas Airways Corporation (BOAC) and from the aviation industry. During the months that followed, the committee met some 60 times and discussed the post-war airliner requirements, in order to advise the government of the types of aircraft that would be needed. The initial report was submitted on 9 February 1943, and it proposed five basic type requirements that the committee considered necessary; a later second report detailed a medium-range airliner of two types, one powered with piston engines and the other with 'propeller-turbines'. The combined reports would ultimately lead to the Airspeed AS 57 Ambassador, Bristol 167 Brabazon, Vickers 630 Viscount, Avro 688 Tudor, Armstrong Whitworth AW 55 Apollo, de Havilland DH104 Dove and the de Havilland DH106 Comet.

The elegant Lockheed Constellation first flew in 1943 and was ideally placed for the post-war airline industry.

Lord Brabazon of Tara chaired the wartime committee that looked into Britain's post-war role in commercial aviation.

At this stage in the war, the Whittle jet engine was still highly classified, and data about its potential was not widely available. One assumes that the committee had most of the information about the turbojet, as it reported that, in its present form, it did not have sufficient power for a transatlantic airliner. Consequently, the turboprop engine was selected to power several of the projects. This is interesting, as the first aircraft powered by turboprops did not fly until September 1945. While the committee retired to consider the turbojet question, Geoffrey de Havilland and his design team, which was under the leadership of R. E. Bishop, had already started to plan for a turbojet-powered airliner. The committee came back with a proposal for a smaller turbojet aircraft, suitable for the Empire and Europe, to carry 14 passengers at 450mph at 30,000ft with a range of 800 miles.

Bishop later wrote: 'The flight trials of the Goblin-engined Vampire in 1943 brought home to us the impressive qualities of speed, smoothness and low cabin-noise level of the jet-powered aircraft and the extreme simplicity of the engine. These qualities were so manifestly desirable for a civil transport that we at Hatfield were led to wonder what price must be paid to achieve them.' The Goblin jet engine was designed by Major Frank Halford and manufactured by de Havilland at Hatfield.

De Havilland came up with some interesting projects; one showed a six-seat twin-boom aircraft with three de Havilland-Halford H2 turbojets mounted at the rear of the fuselage. Another had a canard layout, while a third proposed a tailless aircraft with highly swept-back wings. These concepts remained on paper.

Meanwhile, the committee – of which Geoffrey de Havilland himself was also a member – continued its debate. De Havilland used his influence and his company's expertise with jet aircraft to get the committee to specify a design for a pressurised, transatlantic mailplane that could carry one ton of payload at a cruising speed of 400mph. This challenged the widely held scepticism towards 'fuel-hungry' and 'unreliable' jet engines. The committee accepted the proposal, calling it the 'Type IV' and the MAP awarded a production contract in February 1945 for a 'jet propelled civil transport' to de Havilland under the company designation Type 106.

Out of all the Brabazon designs, the DH106 was seen as the riskiest, both in terms of introducing untried design elements and for the financial commitment involved. De Havilland concentrated on the tailless, swept-back wing design with four engines buried in the wing roots. To gather information on the design concept, permission was granted by the MAP to convert two de Havilland DH100 Vampires with the swept wing as DH108. Design work commenced in October 1945, and three prototypes were built to Specification E.18/45 using standard Vampire fuselages taken from the production line. The new wing was all-metal in construction and attached to the existing pick-up points.

The first prototype DH108, TG283, was completed at Hatfield in the spring of 1946 and taken by road to Woodbridge, Suffolk, where, on 15 May 1946, Geoffrey de Havilland Jr made a few fast taxi runs before taking the aircraft on its first flight. It behaved perfectly and soon entered a test programme. A second aircraft, TG306, joined the test team but broke up on 27 September 1946, killing Geoffrey de Havilland Jr, John Cunningham succeeded him as chief test pilot. Both DH108s had been modified as the test programme proceeded and were used for subsonic work. However, the third example, VW120, was cleared for supersonic flight and, on 9 September 1948, became the first British aircraft to exceed Mach One when flown by John Derry. Later, the surviving DH108s were modified to test the DH106's power controls.

In September 1946, prior to the completion of the DH108s, BOAC requests necessitated a redesign of the DH106 from its previous 24-seat configuration to a larger 36-seat version. Meanwhile, even before the first DH108 had flown, Bishop had come to the conclusion that a tailless passenger aircraft was not the way to proceed, and the design was changed to include a swept-back tailplane. New designs were submitted, and the Ministry of Supply (MoS) ordered two prototypes of the DH106.

Bishop further changed the design and reduced the wing sweepback from 40 degrees to a more conventional 20-degree layout with un-swept tail surfaces married to an enlarged fuselage of 9ft 9in diameter, accommodating 36 passengers in a four-abreast arrangement with a central aisle. Replacing previously specified Halford H1 Goblin engines, four new, more powerful Rolls-Royce AJ65 (later Avon) powerplants were to be incorporated in pairs buried in the wing roots; Halford H2 Ghost engines were eventually applied as an interim solution while the Avons cleared certification.

On 21 January 1947, de Havilland received an Instruction to Proceed from the MoS for the production of two prototypes for the MoS and eight DH106 airliners for BOAC at £450,000 each. This was the first production order placed anywhere for a jet airliner. Shortly afterwards, six DH106s were ordered for British South American Airways (BSAA). The redesigned aircraft was named the DH106 Comet in December 1947. Delivery was projected for 1952.

IMPERIAL AIRWAYS

On 15 July 1919, a de Havilland DH9 belonging to Aircraft Transport and Travel made the first recognised commercial British flight between Hendon and Paris. This flight heralded the start of a scheduled service between the two capitals that got under way in August, but the airline was short-lived and ceased trading in December 1920 when it was bought by Birmingham Small Arms. However, other enterprising businessmen had already formed rival airlines. Handley Page Aircraft used war-surplus Handley Page bombers converted to carry passengers and launched a regular London–Paris service in September 1919; a month later, the company introduced lunch baskets at three shillings (15 pence), becoming the forerunner of in-flight catering. Later, Handley Page Transport extended its schedules to Amsterdam, Basle and Zurich. Aerial transport attracted ship owners S. Instone & Co., and the company began a regular airline service to Paris and later to Cologne. Flying was gaining popularity, and the Daimler Car Company formed Daimler Airways through its Daimler Hire business to fly from London to Berlin via Amsterdam, Bremen and Hamburg.

These pioneer airlines operated on slender margins of profit anyway, but, by the early 1920s, it was clear that assistance was required. The British government stepped in, and Imperial Airways

Handley Page HP42 (G-AAXF) *Helena* getting ready to taxi out at Croydon Airport for a flight to Paris. This aircraft was impressed into RAF service in June 1940.

Short S30 Empire flying boat *Cabot* (G-AFCU) entered airline service in early 1939 and was destroyed by enemy action in May 1940.

was formed on 31 March 1924. The company was formed out of, and took over, the fleets and staff of the existing airlines. Although Imperial Airways maintained a few European services, it concentrated on expanding the Empire routes. By 1927, the company were flying from Basra to Baghdad and Cairo and two years later offered a direct route from Britain to India. Within a few years, Imperial Airways aircraft were operating to Africa, the Far East and Australia (with Qantas taking over in Singapore) and running a service from Bermuda to New York.

In December 1934, the British government announced the Empire Air Mail Programme, which was to commence in 1937. Anticipating the future, the Imperial Airways board ordered a number of Short C-Class flying boats off the drawing board. These elegant aircraft have come to define a special age of luxury travel that was cut short when war was declared in September 1939. Imperial Airways and the private British Airways Limited ceased to exist when they were taken over by the British Overseas Airways Corporation (BOAC) on 1 April 1940.

DE HAVILLAND

Geoffrey de Havilland and his brothers Ivon and Hereward were exceptionally mechanically minded. While attending Crystal Palace Engineering School, Geoffrey built a motorcycle powered by an engine of his own design and used it to commute to and from the family home in Hampshire. By 1906, Geoffrey was designing buses for the Motor Omnibus Construction Company but was also interested in the work of the pioneer aviators in Europe and the US. In 1908, with a loan of £500 from his grandfather, Geoffrey designed a 45hp flat-four water-cooled engine to power an aeroplane of his own construction. However, the first flight in December 1909 was not successful, and the aircraft was wrecked. De Havilland was not injured and immediately commenced building a second aircraft.

On 10 September 1910, Geoffrey's second aircraft made its maiden flight. Then followed passenger flights for his brother-in-law Frank Hearle and for Geoffrey's wife and eight-month-old son, Geoffrey Jr.

By this point, the War Office had become interested in de Havilland's aircraft and invited him to demonstrate it at Farnborough. Suitably impressed, it bought the machine for £400. It also took on de Havilland and Hearle as pilot/designer and mechanic, respectively.

Geoffrey de Havilland designed and flew several aircraft for the newly formed Royal Flying Corps before he left Farnborough to join George Holt Thomas's Aircraft Manufacturing Company (Airco) at Hendon in North London. Here, he designed some of the best-known aircraft – from the DH2 fighter to the DH9 bomber – to see active service during World War One. De Havilland himself was called for service early in the war and was posted to Montrose, but he was more valuable as a designer and was returned to Hendon.

When Airco was bought by BSAA after the war, Geoffrey was offered a job designing motorcars, but he preferred to concentrate on aviation and formed de Havilland Aircraft Company Limited on 25 September 1920. Based at Stag Lane in North London, the small business expanded with financial investment from Alan Butler and became a household name when it produced the DH60G Gipsy Moth, which succeeded in bringing flying to a wider audience. Amy Johnson made headlines when she flew solo from England to Australia in a Gipsy Moth. The series was developed, and most of the RAF pilots of World War Two commenced their basic flying training on the de Havilland Tiger Moth.

Early in World War Two, de Havilland Aircraft started work on a fast, twin-engined light bomber that would be built almost entirely in wood. Ronald Bishop, who had joined de Havilland as an apprentice in 1921, led a design team who worked in secret at Salisbury Hall near the main de Havilland works at Hatfield. Geoffrey de Havilland, Jr. flew the aircraft – now named Mosquito – on 25 November 1940. The Mosquito went into RAF service in 1942 and saw service in all theatres of war from Europe to the Far East.

De Havilland had not been slow to take advantage of the gas-turbine technology and, by 1943, had a small fighter powered by a jet engine designed by Major Frank Halford. Halford's engine was developed and used to power the first Comet airliners. Sir Geoffrey de Havilland died in 1965.

Geoffrey de Havilland.

Geoffrey de Havilland's first aircraft was not a success.

FRANK WHITTLE

The idea of a gas turbine was not new, but it took Frank Whittle, a young RAF officer, to see its potential as a method of propulsion for aircraft. In 1928, while still a cadet, he produced a paper on a practical gas turbine engine, but it was regarded as fanciful and not taken up. However, Whittle was convinced about the theory and patented his design; he also set up a small company, Power Jets, to develop the concept. By the mid-1930s, he had been able to secure limited funding and began the task of manufacturing a jet engine to his design.

This was built by hand at a workshop in Lutterworth and ran for the first time on 12 April 1937. Whittle later recalled:

> [I] opened the control valve when the turbine was turning at 1,000rpm to admit fuel to the pilot burner in the combustion chamber. It all went to plan, and I signalled for an increase to 2,000rpm and then opened the main fuel valve. At first little happened, then, with a rising shriek like an air-raid siren, the speed began to rise rapidly, and large patches of red heat became visible on the combustion chamber casing. The engine was obviously out of control and those present scattered as far as they could from the engine. I closed the valve and stood rooted to the spot. Eventually, the engine ceased revving and shut down. I have rarely been so frightened.

Whittle continued with his experiments, and eventually a version of the Whittle Unit (WU) was built to power the Gloster E28/39 aircraft. On 15 May 1941, this small experimental aeroplane took off from RAF Cranwell and became the first jet-powered aircraft to fly in Britain. In Germany, Pabst von Ohain had designed a gas-turbine engine, and this had been flown in a Heinkel design as early as August 1939 but was not taken up by the Nazi government. Whittle's engine was practical and reliable; it was developed to power the Gloster Meteor, which was the first jet aircraft to enter military service, some months before the German Messerschmitt Me 262.

Major Frank Halford, Chief Engineer of de Havilland Aircraft, was interested in jet power, and, using data from the E28/39, he designed the Goblin engine for de Havilland. This was larger and more powerful than the Whittle unit in the Meteor and was employed to power Britain's second jet fighter, the Vampire.

Frank Whittle was treated shabbily by the post-war Labour government and was sacked from his own company; he later made his home in America, where he was lauded as one of the great innovators of the last century.

Air Commodore Sir Frank Whittle, photographed at Farnborough in 1944. (Rolls-Royce via François Prins)

Chapter 2
Building the World's First Jet Airliner

Work at de Havilland went into top gear; here was an order straight off the drawing board, albeit one that was at a fixed price and subject to a guaranteed delivery date. All of it was in unexplored aviation territory, which was a singularly brave move by de Havilland, albeit one that may have seemed foolhardy at the time. De Havilland constructed two models, one highly accurate scale model for wind tunnel testing and the other a full-size mock-up of the fuselage and inner wing section. Built mainly of plywood, it was utilised to plan the interior layout for the crew and passengers, as well as detailing the engine installations buried in the wing roots.

As chief test pilot, John Cunningham was given responsibility for the emerging airliner. He was detailed to work with BOAC on the ideal cockpit layout for the new aircraft. Cunningham had been a famous night-fighter pilot during the war and was used to military types such as the Mosquito and Beaufighter – the large transport type was new to him. He recalled to this author:

> BOAC operated the best airliner of the time, the Lockheed L049, and their director for the introduction of new aircraft into the fleet, Campbell Orde, told me that I must attend their training facility at Dorval in Canada. So, I went through the course and flew several scheduled North Atlantic flights during the winter of 1946 and 1947 as a crew member, usually second pilot. I spent a month being checked out and also flew the Australia route. The layout of the Comet and the cockpit in particular was determined by the Constellation.

Cunningham also remembered the standards of civilian passenger flying in those immediate post-war years as less than perfect.

> It was very clear from the start that the standards I had through my air force flying were far higher than the pilots I had to fly with. The airline captains flew very well but often thumped their aircraft down rather than making a smooth landing. If we had done that in a squadron, we would be soon told off and made to do the landing again! Some of them were pre-war Imperial Airways captains and that was the way they did it, to be fair they had been used to landing heavy aircraft and flying boats. Anyway, this assisted me enormously with the design for the Comet undercarriage, which had to be made tough to cope with these sorts of landings.

As noted, the design for the flight deck was most important, and much input was gleaned from John Cunningham; what emerged was a smooth nose-section with an excellent view from the flight deck. To arrive at the ideal design, a full-size mock-up was fitted to the nose of Horsa glider (TL348) and towed aloft by Halifax VII PP389 – retained by de Havilland for propeller tests – to find suitable weather and wind conditions for the glider. Cunningham was the usual pilot and made several flights during March and April 1947. The first flight was from nearby Radlett, as Hatfield's runway was being rebuilt. These flights were made to test the efficiency of the DV (direct vision) window and the wipers

A front view of the prototype, taken when it was rolled out at Hatfield before the first flight in July 1949.

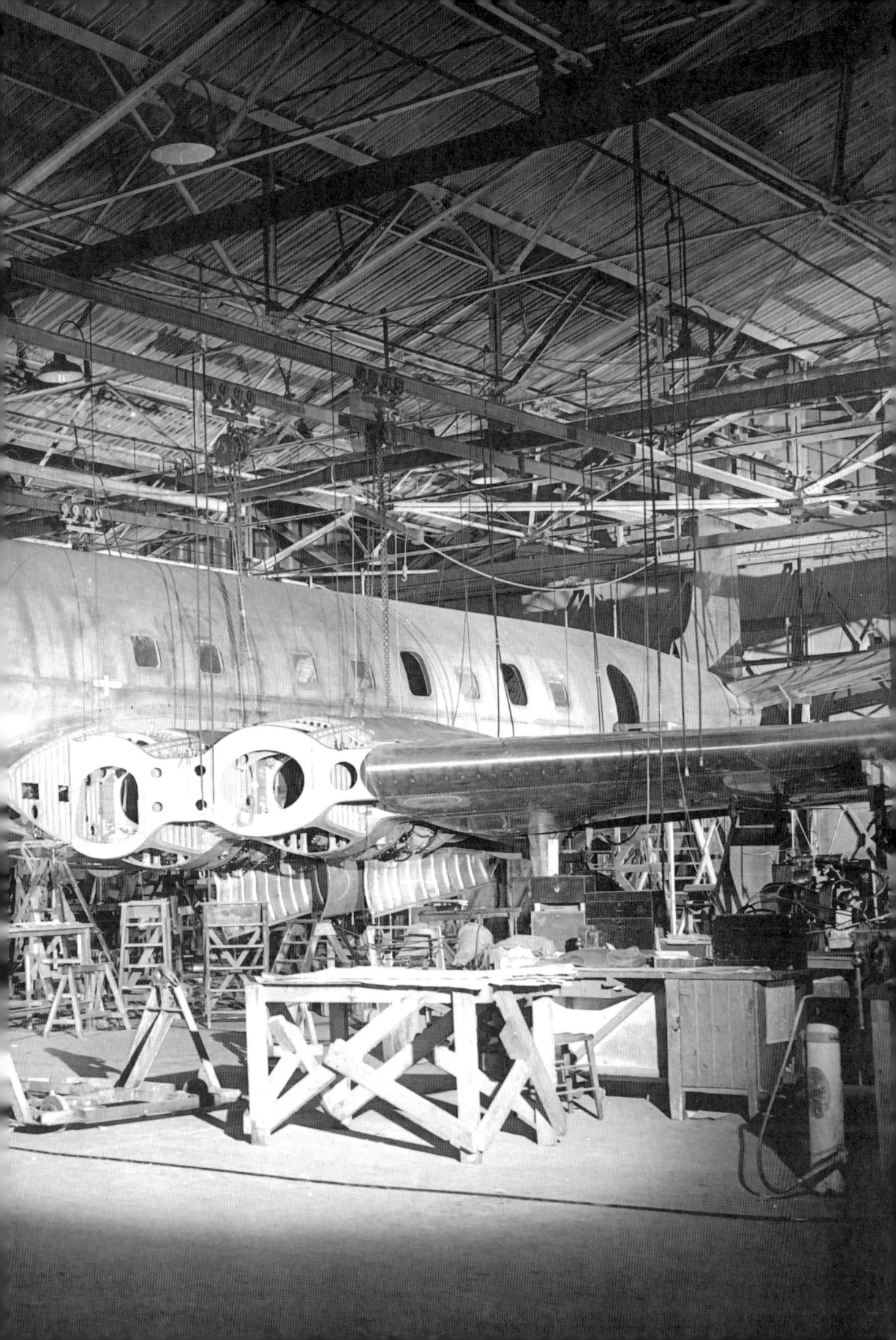

The single mainwheel undercarriage, as seen here, was only fitted to the first prototype Comet.

and for the general view from the flight deck. Cunningham found the Horsa 'very nice to fly' and after several flights in various weather conditions – and some alterations to the design – was satisfied that the general layout could go onto the production DH106. Similarly, he helped with the power-assisted control systems, testing them on a static model and later adding data to the system as fitted to DH108 TG283 for airborne trials, flying for the first time on 11 August 1947. The Lockheed L049 was equipped with partial power controls, whereas the DH106 was to be the first aircraft with total hydraulic power-assisted controls.

If de Havilland based its Comet nose and flight deck on the L049, then Sud Aviation went one better by simply grafting the entire nose of the Comet onto its highly successful and very elegant Caravelle a few years later. Perhaps the feedback from the Air France crews who had flown the Comet 1s was a deciding factor.

On the ground at Hatfield, the testing of all the systems to be fitted to the DH106 continued. Nothing was overlooked, especially the matter of pressurising the fuselage to carry passengers in comfort at 40,000ft, which was, once again, unknown territory. De Havilland built a tank and submerged a complete fuselage while maintaining gentle water pressure until it burst. Noting the breaks, the engineers were able to work on the pressure system. Other trials on the fuselage included extremes of temperature and the ability of the many systems to cope with such extremes. Out of the tank, the fuselage was twisted under pressure to check the strength of the structure. Failures were acted on immediately and newer methods of construction were developed for fitting to the airliner. All aspects were tested in a variety of ways; for example, the nosewheel assembly was mounted on a specially built motorised lorry chassis for steering trials conducted around Hatfield aerodrome.

Engines for the DH106 had first been bench run on 2 September 1945, with promising results. The real test would come in an airborne environment, and for this de Havilland obtained an Avro Lancastrian IV (VM703) and converted it to carry two de Havilland-Halford Ghost engines in place of the outboard Rolls-Royce Merlins. While it would fly on the twin turbines alone once airborne, take-offs, for safety reasons, were with all four engines. Test flying commenced on 24 July 1947, with Cunningham at the controls; later, Chris Beaumont took over some of the testing when another Ghost-Lancastrian (VM729) joined the test programme. Basic data was obtained by these aircraft, but higher altitude performance was necessary, so a Vampire (TG278) was converted to carry the Ghost. This aircraft was modified with extended wingtips and some slight alterations to the fuselage; on 23 March 1948, John Cunningham established a new World Altitude Record of 59,492ft with TG278. At this height, the Ghost performed excellently and led to the development of type for the Venom fighter. To get an idea of the available competition, Cunningham flew some other airliners, including the Avro Tudor. He was quickly able to report that there was nothing even close to the proposed DH106.

While this was going on, the Ministry of Defence looked at the Comet design and concluded that it could be adapted as a bomber, in case the Avro (Vulcan) and Handley Page (Victor) projects being developed to Specification B.35/46 failed. De Havilland were invited to tender and its submission, as DH111, incorporated many Comet features but with a completely redesigned fuselage to carry a 10,000lb bomb load. In the event, the DH111 was rejected by the MoS as being too small, and it ordered prototypes of the Vickers Valiant and Short Sperrin instead. Only the Valiant went into production and RAF service, but the Comet returned as the Nimrod some 20 years later.

From the very start, Cunningham had been involved with the DH106 project and had spent much time building up for when the new aircraft would be ready for test flying. It had been towed out of the factory in April 1949 for successful ground running trials. On the morning of 27 July 1949, the bare metal airliner, carrying the 'B' registration G-5-1 and named 'Comet', was towed out of the flight hangar at Hatfield. Nothing like it had been seen before; it was sleek and really did look like a futuristic shape from the pages of the *Eagle* boys' magazine. Even today, it is still possible to look at a photograph of G-5-1 and marvel at the courage of de Havilland. It was an all-metal 36-seater airliner with a circular fuselage section mounted on a thin wing with four DH Goblin 50s buried in the wing roots. The Comet owed its sleek appearance to the construction method by which the aluminium skins had been attached to the skeleton framework, using a metal cement known as Redux instead of the usual rivets. This saved weight and contributed greatly to a smoother airflow reducing drag.

There had already been engine ground-running and some fast taxi runs up and down the runway, but there had been no checks on the flying controls. On the morning of 27 July, Cunningham

Although not the prototype being built, this shows the rear cabin section of a Comet being mated to the non-pressurised tail section.

decided to make 'three hops to get the feel of the ailerons, elevators and rudder on the Hatfield runway, which was long enough to simply "hop" and recover in time'. Following this, the works took the aircraft away to jack it up and carry out the required checks. These small 'hops' were important, as the Comet was the first British passenger aircraft to be fitted with all-power controls, using the Lockheed Servodyne system, and Cunningham needed to get the 'feel' of the airliner under power, something that could not be simulated. He takes up the story: 'Late in the afternoon, the chief inspector came over and said, "It's yours if you want", so I said, "Yes, let's do the flight now". There were four others: 'Tubby' Waters (co-pilot), John Wilson (electrics), Tony Fairbrother (test observer) and Frank Reynolds (hydraulics).'

Cunningham called the tower and informed them that the Comet (civil registration G-ALVG) was going for take-off. The world's first turbojet airliner took smoothly to the skies, watched by Bishop and a few workers who had stayed behind after work. It was a proud moment, and one that lives on in the minds of those who were present. Cunningham applied power, and the lightly laden natural-metal-finish airliner took off in a short run and climbed out steeply, the single-wheel main undercarriage retracting outwards into bulges under the swept-back wing. Very quickly, 8,000ft was

The engines for the Comet were buried in the wing roots. This gave the airliner a sleek, smooth, uncluttered appearance that still looks good today.

reached, and the aircraft levelled to carry out standard flight tests, stalls (clean and dirty), slow turns and the many other tasks a new aircraft would execute on its first flight. Cunningham recalled:

> I remember that flight quite clearly, as, although I knew we had a powerful aircraft, I did not expect it to accelerate like a fighter! When I throttled back the engines to check the stall, the nose came up and, as expected, she began to shudder, so that was no surprise; you have sufficient warning before the stall. I increased power and pushed the column forwards and the Comet responded as we regained lost height. We also tried a dirty stall with the gear and flaps extended. Again, it was as expected. There were a few niggles that needed to be attended to but very little considering the Comet was all new technology.

Thirty-five minutes later, the Comet landed back at Hatfield to a tremendous welcome. Cunningham takes up the story:

> It was a smooth uneventful flight, and I went home. The next morning Geoffrey de Havilland telephoned me in my office to say that he was delighted with the flight and thanked me for a nice

Lifting of the runway in bright sunshine, the clean lines of the Comet are seen to advantage; note the single mainwheel undercarriage

birthday present. I thought he meant mine, but it was also his birthday and we did not realise it although we had known each other for some years! After that every 27 July he would ring me up and wish me well on my birthday.

John Cunningham did not fly the Comet again until 4 August 1949, when the test programme got under way with several flights a day to build up the necessary hours to show the new airliner at Farnborough. In those balmy days of 1949, there were few, if any, restrictions on flying, and John Cunningham remembered that '...most of the flying was over Norfolk, the Wash and that area, as soon as we took off from Hatfield we headed north-east. There were quite a few American bases and they occasionally they came to see us, but we left them behind as we were much faster than most of the types around!'

Testing of the Comet continued in the coming months, with Cunningham and Peter Bugge sharing the workload. There were very few snags considering the new technology involved. All early flights were carried out unpressurised; the first record of a cabin pressure test appears at 2lb on 27 August.

Carrying the civil registration G-ALVG, the Comet prototype made several proving flights and always attracted a crowd wherever it went.

It was decided to show the aircraft at the SBAC show at Farnborough in September, where, naturally, the all-British airliner dominated and stole the limelight from the 5th to the 12th, when it returned to Hatfield.

Following Farnborough, the Comet was prepared for its first overseas sortie. On the evening of 22 October, Cunningham flew G-ALVG from Hatfield to Heathrow to carry out two night take-offs and landings; the next day he was back at Hatfield. On the 24th, the Comet was airborne for engine checks before a night-flight to Heathrow that evening. Early the next morning, Cunningham and his crew took off from Heathrow, and 3hrs 25mins later, they landed at Castel Benito, Libya. There, they had lunch, refuelled the aircraft and took off to return to Heathrow, where they landed 3hrs 15mins later, before returning to Hatfield that same day. On its first overseas flight, the Comet averaged a speed of 448mph. Fuel consumption figures were acceptable, and the aircraft behaved perfectly. Later that year, Cunningham and the crew carried out a rigorous 5½hr endurance flight around the British Isles; once again, the aircraft performed well, and no snags were detected.

On the ground at Hatfield, modifications were made to the main undercarriage with the substitution of two four-wheel assemblies in place of the single main wheel. The bogie undercarriage was fixed

Taken at Hatfield soon after the first flight, the clean lines of the prototype are seen to their advantage.

down and not retractable, as there was no space in the wing for such an arrangement. The first flight was on 18 December 1949, and subsequent flights were made with different loads to check the performance of the bogie layout. Although the new unit was heavier, the advantages were immediate in braking, taxiing and general handling. It was adopted as standard for the production aircraft.

Comet G-ALVG was refitted with the retractable single-wheel undercarriage and air tested on 11 February 1950, before making another record flight on 16 February, with a Hatfield–Rome–Hatfield flight of 2hrs out and 2hr 5mins back. On 21 February, G-ALVG flew with a cabin pressure of 8,000ft at 40,000ft. No snags were encountered, and in the 11 months following the first flight, the aircraft logged 324 flying hours. Meanwhile, the second Comet prototype (G-5-2/G-ALZK) took shape at Hatfield with several modifications incorporated into the design.

Publicity generated encouraged other airline operators to look at the Comet, and the first to make a decision was Canadian Pacific Airlines (CPA). It ordered ten aircraft as Comet 1As, which had an additional fuel capacity of 1,000 gallons housed in tanks fitted in the wings for the long over-water crossing between Honolulu and Sydney. Other modifications included uprated engines and an increased passenger capacity of 44.

Above: Here, the prototype is at an advanced stage of construction, but the tail section has yet to be joined to the main fuselage.

Right: Another colour picture taken of the Comet prototype being built at Hatfield in 1948.

A rare colour image of the Comet prototype in-build at Hatfield.

There were many VIPs who wished to see and fly in this extraordinary British airliner, and one that John Cunningham remembered with affection bears relating in his own words:

One day in late February DH telephoned me and said 'Is there any chance of fitting a flight in for Lord Trenchard? He is very keen to see the Comet'. Well, I was pleased of course and said 'Yes, anytime he likes'. On March 1, he and Lady Trenchard came to Hatfield and with DH and others [they] climbed aboard. We took off, and there was the old boy happy to be on board, when we were about 40,000ft flying in smooth clear skies he came to the cockpit and leaned over to me. He said, 'I remember in 1912 when I was at Upavon there was a young pilot, called de Havilland, who brought his aeroplane from Farnborough to demonstrate it to us'. That was marvellous as DH was standing behind him and he was my boss, 'young de Havilland!' DH was amused and pleased by this memory, both great men. I remember during the war that Trenchard was always visiting squadrons to see how we were doing.

Flights, such as the above, were fitted into the test flying and the all-important sales programmes of the Comet to other airlines such as Air France, Sabena and KLM.

Exactly a year to the day after G-ALVG had flown, Cunningham and Bugge flew the second aircraft, G-5-2 (G-ALZK), from Hatfield. Many of the modifications dictated from the first aircraft were incorporated, especially the four-wheel bogie main undercarriage, which retracted to lie flush within the mainplane. This arrangement was standard on the production aircraft. Test flying continued until April 1951, when G-ALZK was delivered to the BOAC Comet Unit at Hurn for the airline to carry out flight and cabin crew training. BOAC inaugurated a 500-hour route-proving programme of 12 flights to Johannesburg, Beirut, Delhi, Singapore and Jakarta. These went well, and the airline was keen to see the Comet into service.

In this colour image, the engine covers and intakes have been removed for routine inspection at Hatfield.

From left to right: Major Frank Halford, Lord Trenchard, Lady Trenchard and Geoffrey de Havilland after a flight in the prototype Comet.

JOHN CUNNINGHAM – TEST PILOT

Group Captain John Cunningham CBE, DSO & Two Bars, DFC & Bar, was one of the most famous night-fighter pilots of World War Two. His name will always be associated with de Havilland aircraft and especially with the ground-breaking Comet airliner.

John Cunningham, or 'JC' as he was generally known, was born in Croydon in 1917 to a fairly well-off family; his father was Company Secretary of Dunlop and had an office in St James's. At the age of eight, John attended Whitgift School, near Croydon Aerodrome. These early days of commercial aviation were something of a tonic to young John. 'I loved to see the leviathans of Imperial Airways as much as the speedy fighters visiting the airport from nearby Kenley and Biggin Hill', he told this author. That John was captivated by aeroplanes from the very start is evident, as he would look up whenever one flew overhead. This exasperated his teachers, one of whom told John he hoped that 'an aeroplane would run over you one day!' John knew that his future lay with aviation, but his father was not too keen on JC joining the RAF, so he sought another way.

On leaving school, John applied to de Havilland, and after an interview he was offered a place commencing in the summer of 1935 at Hatfield. About the same time, he heard of a vacancy with 604 Auxiliary Air Force Squadron at RAF Hendon. His application was successful, and he was accepted.

Cunningham in the captain's seat of a Comet on a test flight, with Peter Bugge in the right-hand seat.

John Cunningham and Sir Geoffrey de Havilland after a flight for British Overseas Airways Corporation (BOAC).

John Cunningham and the flight team are greeted by de Havilland workers who had stayed late to see the Comet make its maiden flight on 27 July 1949.

John Cunningham looking out of the cockpit of the prototype Comet before a test flight from Hatfield in 1949. (De Havilland via François Prins)

John Cunningham began his flying training under Hugh David in an Avro 504N and went solo in March 1936; his instructor described him as a 'natural'. The opportunity to test aircraft came when Captain (later Sir) Geoffrey de Havilland suggested that John assist his son, Geoffrey Jr, then chief test pilot, with the test flying of the production DH94 Moth Minor. It was when testing the first Moth Minor off the line that JC had his first and only experience of taking to his parachute. On one flight, in which they came to carrying out spinning tests, the DH94 went into a flat spin and would not be corrected. Both men quickly left the aircraft, which then corrected itself before crashing near Wheathampstead.

During his time with 604 Squadron, JC had been flying the Hawker Demon, often with James 'Jimmy' Rawnsley as his gunner. Early in 1939, the squadron were re-equipped with the Bristol Blenheim Mk I fighter-bomber. As the year progressed, JC divided his time between de Havilland and Hendon, and, on 23 August 1939, the 22-year-old was called for duty when his squadron was posted to RAF North Weald.

War service

The Blenheim I was not suited to night-flying and John remembered that '...the large expanse of Perspex was difficult to keep clean and the very design of the nose glazing meant reflections, however small, were always a problem'. When not on patrol at night, 604 was on escort duty for convoys along the east coast, and it was at North Weald that Cunningham met up with Jimmy Rawnsley once more.

In July 1940, the squadron moved to Middle Wallop for training with the new Airborne Interception (AI) radar then being fitted to the Blenheim. On 2 September 1940, the squadron's Blenheims were replaced with the new Bristol Beaufighter. This aircraft was 'totally different from the Blenheim; it was faster, more responsive and gave the pilot much better vision from the cockpit'. It was in a Beaufighter that John Cunningham and Sergeant Phillipson scored the first night victory using AI, when they shot down a Junkers Ju 88 over Oxfordshire, on a night in November 1940.

Radar demanded different skills from both pilot and operator; they were a team. Guided by ground control radar, the findings were passed to the aircraft operator, who would 'fix' the enemy on his AI screen and vector the pilot towards the trace. While the radar operator could 'see' the enemy on his screen the pilot could not, and to make an accurate attack and to make a conclusive

1949		Type	No.	1st Pilot	or Passenger	(Including Results a
MONTH	DATE					
—	—	—	—	—	—	TOTALS BROUG
July						
	26	Dove	G-ALBM	Self		Landings
	26	Mosquito 38	VT659	Self		+12 2850
	27	Comet	G-5-1	Self	J. Wilson	First Flight
	28	108	VW120	Self		Snag Flight
	28	Vampire	VU190	Self		F.T. Check
	29	108	UW120	Self		To Elmdon
	29	Beaver	G-ALWW	Self		To Hatfield
	29	Vampire	VU190	Self		Elmdon Practice
	30	"	VU190	Self		Kemsley Race

A page from John Cunningham's logbook showing the first flight of the Comet on 27 July 1949. (François Prins)

Group picture at Hatfield with the first Comet 4. Standing in front of the access steps are John Cunningham and Peter Bugge (both with briefcases). (De Havilland via François Prins)

kill, he had to actually see the enemy in reality. The Cunningham-Rawnsley team was very good, and by May 1941, they had shot down 12 confirmed enemy aircraft.

John Cunningham also recalled the time when he was informed by his Commander-in-Chief, Air Marshal Sholto Douglas, that he was to report to the Chief-of-Air Staff, Sir Charles Portal. 'I was quite fearful as for a mere squadron leader to be summoned to the very top was cause for concern', confided John. 'However, my fears were groundless as Geoffrey de Havilland had asked his old friend "Peter" Portal if he could "borrow" me for a particular flight test. I had no idea what it was.' This was for Cunningham to go to Hatfield and fly the prototype Mosquito W4050. John Cunningham was the third pilot to fly the aircraft, and the first service pilot to do so. It was important for de Havilland to obtain the opinion of a serving pilot on how the new aircraft would perform in a combat role. Cunningham was the right man, and on 2 June 1941 – just 18 days after W4052 had first flown – he took it aloft and carried out quite a rigorous flight test. He was highly impressed with the wooden aircraft and turned in a favourable report. 'The Mosquito was a marvellous aircraft and I knew from that first flight that DH had a winner.'

Cunningham was promoted to wing commander and took over 604 Squadron in September 1941; he was also awarded a bar to his DFC. He was then selected to carry out various trials on new and improved radar, with a much more precise search pattern. These trials were concluded in 1942, and he was posted to take charge of the Night Fighting Operational Training Units, based at Cranfield, East Fortune and Charter Hall. In January 1943, Cunningham took command of 85 Squadron at Hunsdon, equipped with the Mosquito. His first interception did not go according to plan. He had been vectored onto the tail of a Dornier Do 217 and closed in to carry out a kill. Pressing the firing button, nothing happened; he tried again with no result. On landing, an inspection showed an electrical fault with the firing mechanism.

The late HM Queen Elizabeth, the Queen Mother, being escorted by Cunningham at the Mosquito Museum in 1990. (David Oliver)

In March 1944, John was promoted to group captain and posted to 11 Group, where he took over Night Operations. When the war ended, he thought about staying on in the service, but Geoffrey de Havilland offered him a job at Hatfield as chief test pilot of the engine division, a post he took up at the end of 1945.

Post-war test pilot

When Geoffrey de Havilland Jr was killed while flying the experimental DH108 on 27 September 1946, John was appointed chief test pilot. De Havilland took a tremendous gamble when it decided to build the world's first turbo-jet powered airliner – the Comet – and Cunningham was given the task of seeing the project through. He was involved in every aspect of the new airliner, and, on 27 July 1949, he took off from Hatfield in the world's first jet airliner.

His job was not all Comet flying, as in his capacity of chief test pilot, Cunningham was also responsible for other de Havilland designs. However, he continued to test the Comet as it progressed to the definitive Comet 4 and entered BOAC service. In December 1958, he was made a director of de Havilland and was involved in discussions with British European Airways (BEA) regarding de Havilland's new airliner, for which BEA had issued a specification in 1956. The resulting DH121 (later Trident) was chosen by BEA and ordered in quantity production from the drawing board, without the need for a prototype.

Early in August 1961, the first DH121 Trident was completed, and JC carried out ground trials at Hatfield. On 9 January 1962, Cunningham was at the controls of the Trident for its maiden flight. He continued with the flight test programmes and led the team testing de Havilland-Hawker Siddeley and (later) British Aerospace products.

John retired from flying in 1977 but was as busy as ever with many activities linked to the RAF and the aviation industry. He was Chairman of the Trustees of the Geoffrey de Havilland Flying Foundation and attended the annual awards ceremony to present the Foundation's Achievement Medals. He never lost his enthusiasm for aviation and was always a valued and honoured guest at many events he attended.

John fell ill late in 2001 and died a week short of his 85th birthday on 21 July 2002. Since 2004, the Air Squadron has administered John Cunningham Flying Scholarships, funded in part by his estate. John Cunningham will never be forgotten and remains one of the great aviators.

COMET BUILD AT HATFIELD

Chapter 3

Into Passenger Service

While G-ALZK was working with BOAC, G-ALVG was continuing trials with de Havilland for the MoS; records were broken when Cunningham flew the aircraft between London and Copenhagen. The aircraft took it all in its stride, cold weather did not bother the Ghosts, and the next stage was high, hot climates for further trials. G-ALVG flew to Khartoum and then to Nairobi, both airports high and hot! Apart from a small undercarriage malfunction, no problems were encountered. BOAC handed back G-ALZK to de Havilland in October as it waited for the first production aircraft to be delivered.

Passengers and guests board Comet 1 G-ALYP at London Heathrow on 2 May,1952, for the world's first scheduled passenger flight by a jet airliner.

Air France's first Comet 1A, F-BGNX, photographed in colour on a pilot training flight before delivery.

Comet 1 G-ALYX wearing a slightly modified BOAC main title, which was changed in due course.

The first production Comet 1 (G-ALYP) made its maiden flight from Hatfield on 9 January 1951; it was powered by four de Havilland-Halford Ghost 50 Mk 1 engines. G-ALYP differed little from the prototypes but had a slight increase in area to the rudder and wing fences to improve stall characteristics. A test programme commenced before the aircraft was delivered to BOAC for its own trials pending introduction into service.

Early in January 1952, G-ALYP was accepted by the airline, but the first full Certificate of Airworthiness for revenue flights went to G-ALYS on 22 January, and the airline commenced simulated passenger flights carrying freight to Johannesburg. On 2 May 1952, Comet G-ALYP, under the command of Fleet Captain Alistair Majendie and with 36 souls on board, made the world's first scheduled passenger service by a jet airliner from London to Johannesburg. The Comet flew via Rome, Beirut, Khartoum, Entebbe and Livingstone to Johannesburg, where it touched down 23½hrs after leaving Heathrow. During the 6,774-mile flight, the aircraft had behaved perfectly, with the fare-paying passengers and VIPs on board unanimous in their praise for a smooth and comfortable flight.

Britain had left the competition behind; the nearest rival was Boeing's Dash-80, which was still on the drawing board. BOAC quickly established the Comet routes and was the envy of the world. By August, BOAC commenced a regular service between London and Colombo, then on to Karachi and Singapore, and, by the following year, Tokyo had been added to the schedules. The Comet flew regularly with high load factors, generally 32 out of 36 seats were filled on each flight.

De Havilland showed Comet 1A CF-CUM, the first for Canadian Pacific, at Farnborough in September 1952, and this, along with the BOAC scheduled flights, encouraged other airlines. Air France ordered three (F-GBNX–NZ); Union Aeromaritime de Transport also ordered three

Another view of Air France F-BGNX on a training flight.

The first Comet built for Air France landing back at Hatfield after its first test flight.

Two modes of transport centuries apart — BOAC Comet 1 G-ALYU posed in Khartoum with some local camels for a press opportunity.

A Royal Canadian Air Force Comet of 412 Transport Squadron is seen after making the first jet transport flight across the Atlantic.

A Comet prototype, still in bare metal finish but carrying the civil registration G-ALVG, Union flag and the BOAC speedbird motif.

Canadian Pacific Comet 1A CF-CUN is seen at a misty airport with a Pan American DC-4 at the right.

The Comet is waved off from Heathrow en route to Johannesburg.

(F-BGSA–SC) and the Royal Canadian Air Force purchased two examples. The latter's aircraft became the first jet transport to cross the Atlantic during delivery to No 412 Squadron on 29 May 1953. Air France operated its first Comet flight from Paris to Beirut via Rome using F-GBNY on 26 August 1953.

It is worth noting that de Havilland fitted Sprite rockets to G-ALVG for assisted take-off tests with a heavy load and/or on short runways, and as such it was demonstrated at the SBAC show at Farnborough, where it ended its days as a test vehicle before being broken up in 1953.

At this stage, future prospects for the Comet looked good, but then the first problems began to appear. On 26 October 1952, G-ALYZ, under the command of Captain Harry Foot, was on the last leg of Flight BA115 from Johannesburg, when it was damaged beyond repair on take-off from Rome-Ciampino airport.

At 1858hrs, the tower gave G-ALYZ take-off clearance, and the aircraft taxied out in a steady drizzle towards the runway. Harry Foot eased the brakes off and increased power, quickly reaching 80kts and raising the nose; the aircraft swung slightly towards starboard, and the pilot corrected this. At 112kts, the airliner became airborne, but almost immediately the port wing dropped, and the aircraft turned to port, the pilot regained control and noted that they were not building up any speed. Captain Foot eased the control column forwards, by now the Comet was juddering – signifying the stall – and moments later it fell back on the runway, the undercarriage was still down. It was too late to abandon take-off; the aircraft struck the end of the runway and careered onto the soft ground beyond and skidded for some 300 yards before coming to rest. The wing tank had been ruptured, and fuel spilled around the wreck; fortunately, there was no fire, and all 35 passengers and the crew were unhurt. Subsequent investigation showed that the tail of the Comet had scraped along the runway, the nose was too high, and the wing was partially stalled. Harry Foot was blamed for the incident and transferred to BOAC freight operations.

Naturally, de Havilland were concerned and instigated tests at Hatfield – John Cunningham recalled:

> I used to demonstrate on the main runway what Harry Foot had done by putting the tail on the ground; you could recover by putting the nose down again and building up speed to lift off. The older propeller-trained pilots relied on the slipstream from the propellers to literally drag the aircraft off the ground. This is not a criticism as that was what most of heavy bomber pilots did, but with a jet there is no slipstream to give additional lift. So, we modified the underside of the fuselage with a wooden skid and [as a demonstration] I would scrape the Comet along before carrying out the recovery.

The centre console of a Comet being checked at Hatfield.

The second prototype Comet (G-ALZK) being manufactured at Hatfield.

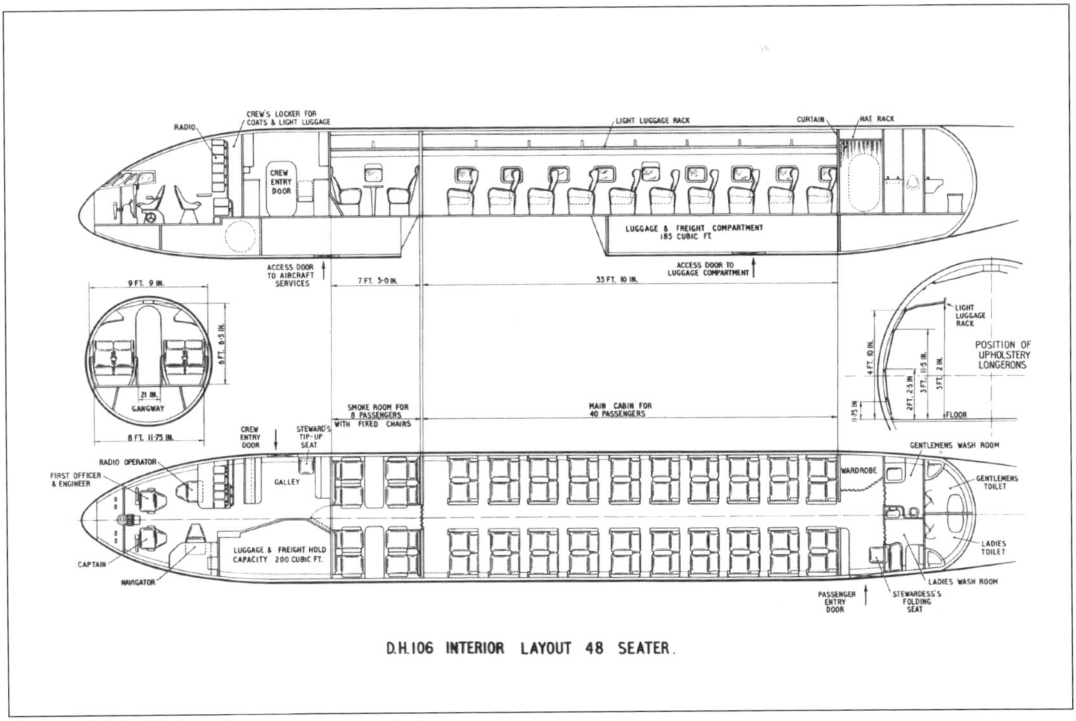

D.H.106 INTERIOR LAYOUT 48 SEATER.

The original layout for the 48-seater BOAC Comets.

Above: Comet 2 interior.

Left: Comet 2 first Class cabin, which included four-seats with a table.

Chapter 4

Comet 1 Problems

Crashes and Farnborough investigations

On 31 December 1952, Cunningham test flew Comet 1A CF-CUN *Empress of Hawaii* at Hatfield before delivery to CPA. Captain Charles Pentland, who had been Chief Instructor at Dorval, took command as CPA's training pilot. Not long after the aircraft entered service, disaster struck on 13 March 1953, when CF-CUN, under the command of Pentland, crashed at Karachi on take-off en route to the service base at Sydney from where it was to commence CPA's service across the Pacific to Honolulu and Vancouver. It was a similar incident to that of G-ALYZ, but unfortunately, the CPA aircraft burst into flames and killed the 11 CPA crew and technicians on board. John Cunningham remembered the incident very clearly:

> BOAC rang up Hatfield about one a.m. and they rang me to say that a seat was booked on the overnight flight on an Argonaut to Karachi and would I please go out. This was the first news I had of the Comet crash.
>
> Well, I went and on arrival met a BOAC captain who had witnessed the crash. He was passing through and wanted to see the Comet take off and recalled that he saw sparks from the runway

A steel water tank was erected around BOAC Comet 1 G-ALYU at Farnborough. The rubber seal fitted around the wing roots is clearly visible in this image.

and then the whole aircraft went up in flames. I walked out to the runway and saw the marks and knew exactly what it was. I had shown Rodley, the BOAC chap, what a ground stall attitude was and what action to take. We could see the point at which the nosewheel had come back down to the runway, but it was too late and it hit a stone bridge and the rising ground at that point.

Pentland had seen the demonstrations at Hatfield, but rather tragically he only remembered the correcting actions too late to save the aircraft and the lives of those on board. Ronald Bishop and his team worked to make the aircraft safe with the tail on the ground and redesigned the leading edge of the wing to give more lift; this cured that problem, but worse was to come. The official report questioned the wisdom of the captain – who had limited experience with the Comet – in taking off with an aircraft at its maximum permissible weight. It added that the recommended take-off procedure as laid-down by the manufacturer had not been adhered to. Until the new wing modifications could be carried out, the take-off and landing speeds were raised to avoid risk of stalling and a repeat of the CPA accident.

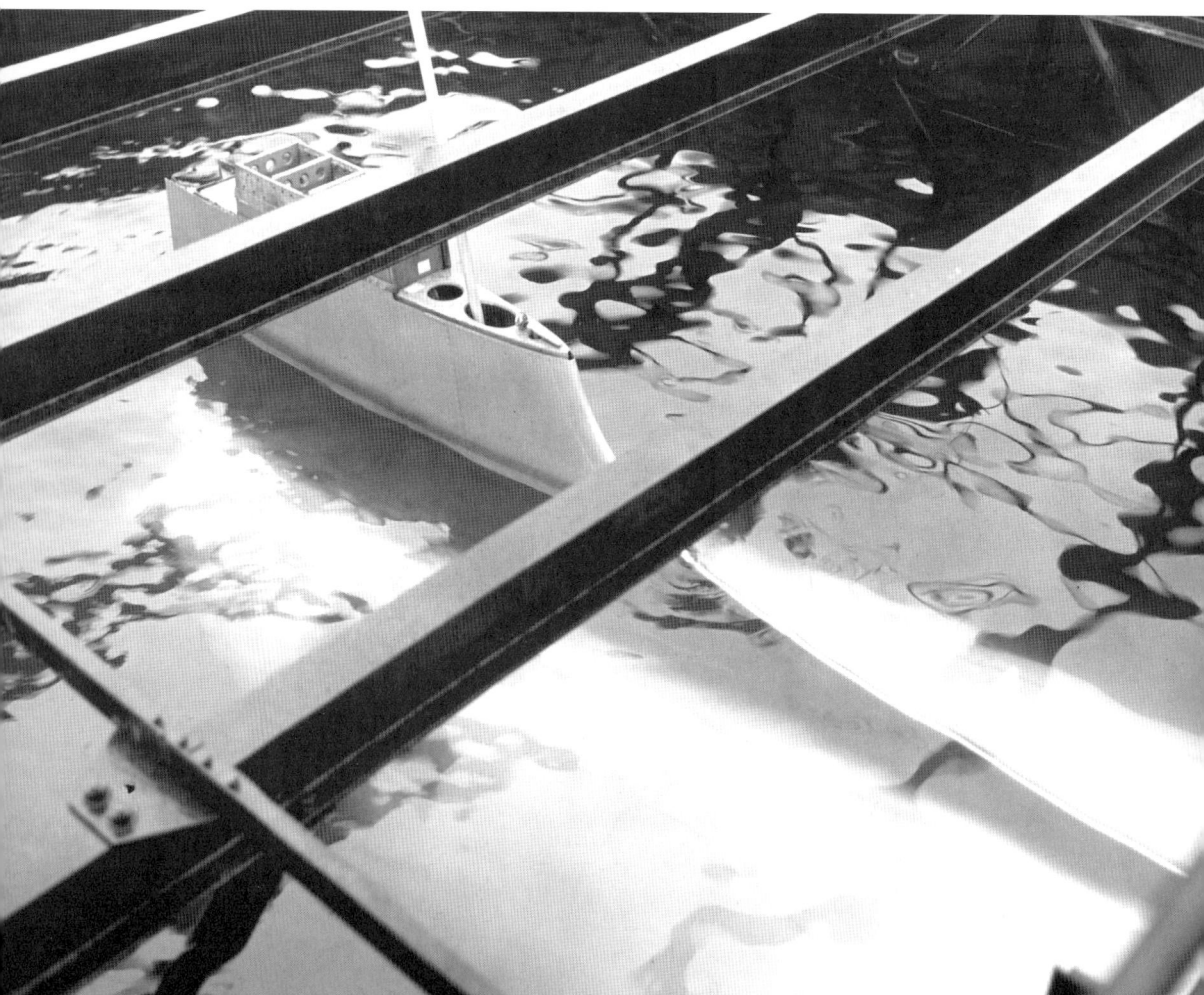

The tail of BOAC Comet 1 G-ALYU was submerged in a specially built tank at Farnborough during the investigations.

Arnold Hall and his colleagues examine a scale model of a Comet 1 during the crash investigation hearings in London.

Canadian Pacific sold CF-CUM to BOAC as G-ANAV to replace the destroyed G-ALYZ. Just three months later, on 25 June 1953, Air France also suffered when F-BGSC was damaged beyond repair at Dakar, Senegal, in a similar accident. These incidents clearly showed that if the nose was too high during take-off, the aircraft would not reach flying speed.

On 2 May 1953 – a year after the first scheduled flight – BOAC Comet G-ALYV was being flown out of Calcutta en route for Delhi by Captain Haddon when the aircraft crashed while climbing to altitude, killing 43 people on board. Unfortunately, in those days, no weather radar was fitted to the Comet and Haddon had taken off into extreme turbulence. When the aircraft was overdue, ground and air searches were instigated. The following morning, the crew of a BOAC York freighter, flown by Captain Foot (ironically the captain of G-ALYZ, which crashed in Rome), spotted the wreckage of the missing G-ALYV scattered over a large area. When local eyewitnesses were questioned, they related seeing a burning wingless aircraft plummeting earthwards through the rainstorm. It later transpired that the wing had failed in download, and the aircraft was lost. There was nothing Haddon could have done, except to have cancelled the flight because of the weather. Following this incident, later-build Comets were fitted with weather radar as standard.

As much of the wreckage that could be collected was sent back to England for examination by the Royal Aircraft Establishment (RAE) at Farnborough. The experts laid the sections out in their correct positions on the floor of a hangar and began the mammoth task of trying to discover how each piece

Some of the wreckage recovered by the Royal Navy is seen here being examined during the hearings at Church House, Westminster, London.

had broken away and fallen. They concluded that the Comet had suffered a structural failure probably due to the adverse weather conditions. They did not find fault with the basic design or build of the aircraft.

Then, on 10 January 1954, G-ALYP, under the command of Captain A. Gibson DFC, took off from Rome at 1100hrs and began to climb to cruising altitude above the cloud layer. The Comet sped ahead and passed weather reports to a BOAC Argonaut that had taken off earlier from Rome. During the transmission, in the middle of a sentence, the radio suddenly went dead. Below the clouds some fishermen, in the sea near Elba, heard the engines of the Comet as it passed overhead followed by the sound of multiple explosions; as they looked up, they saw several sections of burning debris falling through the low cloud. The fishermen, who had been joined by other boats, immediately searched the area and recovered 15 bodies and some sections of the Comet, the rest of which lay in 400ft of water. All 29 passengers and six crew were killed.

Investigations began immediately into the crash, and the search continued to recover as much wreckage as possible. BOAC and Air France grounded their Comets to carry out checks into the structure, hydraulics, electrical and control systems, as well as the general overall condition of each aircraft. The various investigations proved inconclusive, and on 23 March, the aircraft were returned to service. The decision was to prove tragically wrong.

During the inspection, the opportunity was taken to incorporate over 50 modifications to each airliner. While the Comets were on the ground, the Royal Navy was busy recovering the wreckage, which was strewn over a large area of the seabed. It was a long and slow process, but the search yielded most of the surviving parts of G-ALYP.

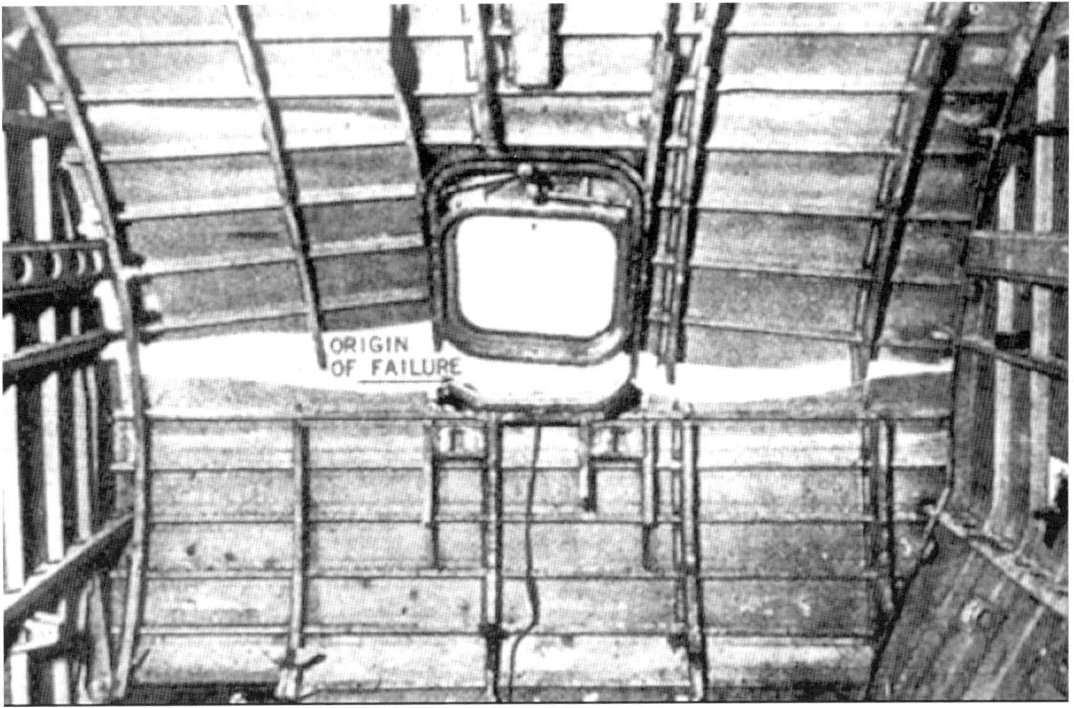

Above and below: Exterior and interior photos showing the point at which the Comet fuselage burst during the water tank tests at Farnborough.

ORIGIN
OF FAILURE

Canadian Pacific bought two Comet 1As from de Havilland but lost one in an accident at Karachi.

On 8 April, Comet G-ALYY, flown by Captain W. Mostert, took off from Rome and began to climb; it crashed off Stomboli, killing 21 people on board. HMS *Eagle*, which happened to be in the vicinity, picked up bodies and some wreckage from the sea for return to Britain. Unlike G-ALYP, there was no opportunity of diving on the wreck, as the waters were too deep and dangerous, although HMS *Eagle* remained on station and continued to search for bodies and wreckage.

The Comet fleets in Britain, Canada and France were grounded immediately; those aircraft not at their home bases were flown back to base by volunteer crews in easy stages at low weights, at an altitude below 20,000ft. Initial investigations showed no mechanical or structural defects.

Two aircraft were allocated to de Havilland and three to the RAE at Farnborough for investigation into the crashes. Led by Arnold Hall (later Sir Arnold), the task has entered the history books as one of the largest and most comprehensive to have been carried out.

At Farnborough, a large water tank was built around a BOAC Comet (G-ALYU) fuselage, which enabled the entire aircraft to be submerged under water; the wings stuck out either side through watertight rubber seals. It was impressive to say the least, as 250,000 gallons were pumped into the tank, filling the cabin and covering the aircraft. Water pressure in the cabin was raised, held and lowered to represent climb, cruise and descent conditions; each five-minute cycle was equivalent to a three-hour flight. At the same time, the wings were heaved up and down by rams to simulate wind gusts in flight. This went on for six-weeks, non-stop, to find the suspected cause of the crashes. Other aspects were not neglected, and Hall's team continued to probe the wreckage of G-ALYP being brought to Farnborough and slowly being assembled onto a wooden frame, or at least as much as was recovered by the Royal Navy, which did a magnificent job. Fortunately, the navy had a trawler in the area and literally 'trawled' for wreckage on the sandy seabed. To assist, several models of the Comet were used to establish where the wreckage would fall. Nothing was spared, and underwater television cameras were also pressed into use to locate important components from the aircraft.

Many other conditions were also investigated. Models were made to simulate some possible causes; dummies were dropped from aircraft flying at various altitudes – this after medical evidence at the inquest on recovered bodies. Comets were flown by test pilots on oxygen without cabin pressurisation at high altitude and top speed to check for pilot mishandling; the test pilots were encouraged to push the Comet to the limit. Most of the flying was carried out with G-ANAV. Flying alongside, photographing and checking the trials, was an RAF Canberra. These tests all proved inconclusive – meanwhile, G-ALYU continued to rumble underwater as two sisters (G-ALYR and 'YS) were ground tested for fatigue.

Finally, after a simulated 9,000hrs flying, the pressure gauges suddenly flicked back to zero – the fuselage had failed. About the same time, the team working on the wreckage of G-ALYP made a startling discovery. There were marks on the wings made by parts of the cabin blowing out and getting caught by the slipstream. The breaks in the fuselage all led back to where one of the automatic direction finders (ADF) had been fitted on the forward cabin roof. The call went out for the missing cabin section to be found, as it was now apparent that the cabin had failed first. Searching continued, and in mid-August, the missing section was located, showing the metal failure at the rear ADF window. Farnborough had solved the problem, and a full report was prepared for the Court of Enquiry, which was held in October.

No blame was attached to the manufacturer, as it had built the aircraft following known engineering principles; it was commended in its work to correct the weaknesses of the design and were encouraged to develop the design. With the benefit of hindsight – always dangerous – it would appear that British aviation was damaged by the highlighting of the disaster while no mention was made of the tremendous steps forward taken by de Havilland and others at the time. It also gave the rival manufacturers across the Atlantic more time and even more valuable material to benefit from, as the findings were made public.

Chapter 5

Comet 2, 2E and 3

Entry into the RAF

while the Comet 1 was entering airline service, de Havilland were already at work developing the type for the transatlantic route, as the Comet 1's range was insufficient. To test the more powerful Rolls-Royce Avon 502 engines, Comet 1 G-ALYT was modified during build and flew as the Comet 2X from Hatfield on 16 February 1952. Other modifications included an additional fuel capacity to 7,000 gallons and a 3ft fuselage extension. Later, an Avon was fitted to the aircraft in the outboard starboard position with a water spray rig at the intake. This was used in trials to develop an ice protection system in the engine and an intake for the Comet 4.

With the initial success of the Comet 1, the Comet 2 was being developed and BOAC placed an order for 12 44-seat examples for its South American routes. Its first aircraft, G-AMXA, flew on

BEA Comet 4B at Moscow airport. The RAF made its first operational Comet flight to Moscow on 23 June 1956.

An RAF Comet C2 (XK696) in formation with Comet C4 (XR397) in 1962. The C4 later became G-BDIU with Dan Air.

27 August 1953, and its appearance at Farnborough did help to lift the gloom hanging over the type. Learning from the Comet 1 disasters, the fuselages of the new aircraft were rebuilt at Chester using heavier gauge metal. In many ways, it was a total redesign. However, although production was halted on the Comet 2 while the investigations were underway, the Comet 3 prototype (G-ANLO) was proceeded with and first flown by Cunningham and Bugge on 19 July 1954. This aircraft was destined to be a 'one-off'. Powered by Rolls-Royce Avon 502 engines, it was fitted with pinion tanks at two-thirds of the wingspan and had passenger accommodation for 78.

Despite the fact that the Comet's future was still uncertain, the go-ahead with the Comet 3, which was just 15ft longer than the Comet 2, meant that it was greeted with great enthusiasm when it appeared at Farnborough and confirmed that, even though some exhibitors may have been in competition, the British aviation family was firmly supporting de Havilland. John Cunningham explained:

It was heartening and very encouraging. Even though they may have been rivals, people like Sir Thomas Sopwith and Sir Frederick Handley Page had come the same route as Geoffrey

A fine air-to-air image of Comet C2R (XK697) from RAF Transport Command, taken in 1956.

de Havilland. They were all pioneers and here was Sir Geoffrey bravely showing Comet 3, even though the investigations on the Comet 1 crashes was on-going. The results were shared, and the entire aircraft business benefited from our problems. I knew that Sir Geoffrey was going through the most awful time, but he never blamed anyone, he just wanted to get to the heart of the problem and rectify it. He was an inspiration to us all, certainly to me.

It is well worth noting that Sir Miles Thomas and the BOAC board never lost faith in the Comet and supported de Havilland all through the investigations into the Comet accidents.

Following the investigations, Comet 1s were mostly taken over by the government for use as test aircraft; they were too valuable to consign to the fire dump or scrapman. Meanwhile, the Comet 2 was undergoing stringent tests, including a civilian passenger-carrying Certificate of Airworthiness – unusual for an aircraft destined for RAF service, but the manufacturers were taking no chances. Testing continued, and in May 1956, the Comet 2 was given a clean bill of health for the RAF, which had ten aircraft on order, pioneering the use of a pure-jet for military transport duties.

Comet T2 XK669 of 216 Squadron was named *Taurus* in 1959 and served until 1966, when it was withdrawn from use.

RAF Transport Command's first
Comet T2 (XK669) was delivered
in June 1956 to RAF Lyneham.

The RAF required ten high-speed aircraft for Transport Command and three for special duties with 51 Squadron. De Havilland Comets entered RAF service with 216 Squadron on 7 July 1956, when XK670 arrived at Lyneham. Along with XK669, these were designated Comet T2s and used for crew training before eight Comet C2s – fitted with 44 seats – arrived for normal transport duties. These were a great success with the RAF and were the first to be fitted with Rolls-Royce Avon 117s in place of the Ghost. Three other specially equipped ex-civilian Comet 2s – XK655, XK659 and XK663 – were modified by Marshalls of Cambridge for use by 51 and 192 squadrons. The first operational flight of a Comet by 216 Squadron was on 23 June 1956, when it carried the then-air minister to Moscow for the Soviet Air Force Day celebrations. They continued to set records as the first military jet transport squadron in the world with such flights as Lyneham to Adelaide in 38hrs. The Comet's speed made it invaluable in its transport role and also during subsequent emergencies in Suez and Cyprus. Comets of 51 and 192 squadrons also played an important role during the missile testing programme at Woomera, Australia, and during the H-bomb trials on Christmas Island in the Pacific. Just over five years after the C2 entered service, 216 Squadron received its first Comet C4 in February 1962 when XR395 and XR399 arrived. For the military-configured C4, there were 94 rearwards-facing passenger seats, and to give Transport Command more scope, the aircraft were easily convertible into ambulances, each with 12 stretchers, 47 seats for injured and space for six medical attendants. If required, the RAF Comets could also be quickly converted to VIP configuration. The two versions of the Comet flew side by side until the C2s were retired in April 1967. The military C4 continued to fly until 30 June 1975, when defence cuts took it out of service some years before it was due to be retired. VC-10 aircraft then took over the Comet's duties.

Comet 2E and Comet 3

Meanwhile, the Comet 3, with the flight team led by Cunningham and Bugge, was fully occupied with route-proving trials for the planned Comet 4, with a marathon around-the-world flight, in December 1955, via Cairo, Bombay, Singapore, Darwin and Sydney. At the last location, Australians welcomed the aircraft with a large crowd of some 35,000 people, who actually mobbed the aeroplane until police moved them with the use of water cannons. Flight time had been 24hrs 30mins. Onwards the aircraft flew, on to London via New Zealand and North America. After 30,000 miles, the aircraft was serviceable; there had been no problems, everything had worked superbly. It was the first encirclement of the globe by a jet airliner, and there could have been no better vindication for the excellence of de Havilland, Rolls-Royce and the many other suppliers.

BOAC, which had added five Comet 3s to the order, cancelled all until the outcome of the Farnborough inquiry. It now placed a £34m order for 19 Comet 4s, and G-ANLO was further modified to be more representative of the model. More powerful Avon 523s dictated the rebuilding of the engine bays, and some work was carried out on the wingtips. About this time, BEA were aware of the need for a pure-jet aircraft; on the drawing board was the DH121 (later Trident), but this was quite far in the future. As a stop-gap, in September 1957, BEA placed an order for six, later increased to 14, 100-seat Comet 4Bs to commence operations in 1960.

Comet 3/4 G-ANLO carried out several further trials for the proposed Comet 4 before being given the service serial XP915 and joining the RAE at Bedford for Blind Landing Experiments in June 1961. Also used on similar trials, although for the civilian manufacturer Smiths, was Comet 2E G-AMXK. Later, this aircraft was taken over by the MoS as XV144, and from November 1966, it was also used

The sole Comet 3 built was used extensively as a test aircraft for the Comet 4 programme.

by the Blind Landing Experimental Unit at Bedford. Two aircraft (G-AMXD and XK) were modified as Comet 2Es for work on the proposed Comet 4. More powerful Rolls-Royce Avon Mk 524 RA29 engines were installed in the outboard engine bays and Avon 504s in the inner; an exhaustive test programme was initiated. BOAC took over the two aircraft after de Havilland had completed its trials and flew them on typical airline routes between London, Beirut and Calcutta as a prelude to the introduction of the Comet 4.

By June 1958, G-AMXK began a series of transatlantic proving flights in a programme of three phases. First, 11 one-day return flights to Gander via Keflavik. Then eight three-day journeys (the first day to Gander, the next from Gander to Goose, Stephenville, Sydney and Moncton and return to Gander and lastly, the return to London). The third phase consisted of eight further flights to Gander on day one, with the next day spent practising approach and let-down procedures at Baltimore, Montreal, Boston and New York before returning to Gander and flying back to London at the end of the phase. In all, BOAC flew 3,850hrs on Comet 2Es, of which 423 were on the North Atlantic crossing.

John Cunningham and Peter Bugge displayed the Comet 3 (G-ANLO) at Farnborough.

Comet 3 prototype (G-ANLO) and Comet 2E (AMXD) seen at Farnborough in 1955. Both aircraft wear BOAC livery, but the Comet 3 never flew with the airline.

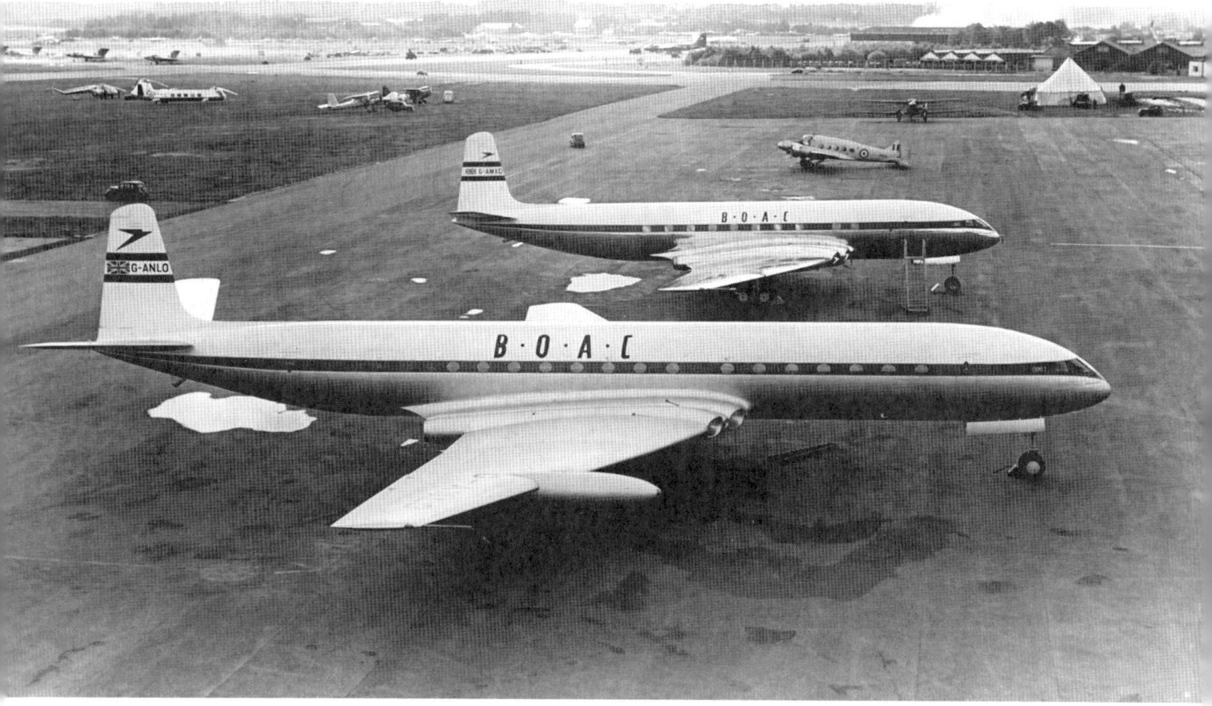

Chapter 6
Comet 4 and Airline Service

World beater

In early summer 1956, de Havilland announced the Comet 4A, which was suited for short- and medium-range operations up to a maximum distance of 2,500 statute miles. This version was longer than the Comet 3 and could seat 92 passengers, five abreast, in comfortable seats. A few weeks later, on 24 July 1956, de Havilland and Capital Airlines in the US jointly announced the purchase of 14 Comets, with four Comet 4s being delivered by the end of 1958, followed by ten Comet 4As in the second half of 1959. Capital aircraft would have 74 passengers in four abreast seating.

The comprehensive test programme with the Comet 3 and the various Comet 2s meant that, when the Comet 4 was offered, it was fully developed and ready for airline use. After all of that development and a great deal of redesigning, the Comet 4 prototype (G-APDA) was flown for the first time on 27 April 1958, with Cunningham and Bugge as pilots. Almost immediately, the aircraft embarked

United Arab Airlines ordered nine examples of the Comet 4C, which operated from Cairo to Europe, India, Japan and East and West Africa.

Compagnia Mexicana de Aviacion operated the Comet 4C on internal routes as well as to North America.

on a series of long-range flights, breaking records along the way. Among the flights was one on 14 September, when the aircraft was flown the 7,925 miles from Hong Kong to London in a flying time of 16hrs 16mins. Three days later, G-APDA flew from London to Gander in 5hrs 47mins, and then on successive days proceeded to make further non-stop flights from Montreal–Vancouver–Mexico City–Lima–Buenos Aires.

It was a great moment when BOAC inaugurated the first transatlantic crossing by fare-paying passengers on a jet airliner. This was made simultaneously on 4 October 1958 by G-APDC from Heathrow (Captain Roy Millichap) and G-APDB from New York (Captain Tom Stoney). Soon, BOAC introduced the Comet 4 onto all major routes, and passengers took to them with great alacrity, all the troubles from a few years before totally forgotten. Comet had beaten Pan American and its Boeing 707 with the first crossing of the Atlantic. It also beat them with the first jet airliner crossing of the Pacific Ocean. Within 18 months, BOAC Comets were flying to all six continents, and it was the first jet airliner to operate in Latin America.

BOAC Comet 4s continued to give exceptional service until they were retired in 1965, and the larger VC10 and Boeing 707s replaced them on all routes. In 1966, five ex-BOAC Comets were sold to Malaysian Airways, two went to Mexicana, two to Dan-Air, one to Ecuador and one on a six-month lease to East African Airways (EAA). The remainder of the fleet, which were parked outside BOAC's engineering hangar at Heathrow Airport, were advertised for sale at £500,000 each.

Variants of the definitive Comet 4 served in several liveries. Most famous, however, are the BOAC Comet 4s; these had a wingspan of 114ft 10in and a length of 111ft 6in and were fitted with Rolls-Royce Avon 524 engines. For shorter routes, a version with 7ft off the wingspan and 7ft added to the fuselage was produced, enabling higher cruising speeds and lower altitudes. Initially, as noted earlier, Capital Airlines ordered such a variant, but a policy change meant the order was cancelled and

BEA operated several examples of the Comet 4B; one is seen here refuelling at Porto Santo, Portugal.

BEA took up the aircraft. Once again, Comet 3 G-ANLO was used as the test-vehicle with shortened wingspan and flew as Comet 3B on 21 August 1958. The first aircraft for BEA, G-APMA, commenced certification trials in June 1959, which included being loaned to BEA for the London to Paris air race the following month.

BEA took delivery of its first Comet 4B on 9 November 1959, when G-APMB arrived at Heathrow, with G-APMC following a week later. Proving flights commenced, after some delays, on 5 December, when G-APMB flew to Moscow and later to other destinations. On occasion, the Comet replaced Viscounts on commercial flights before entering scheduled services on 1 April 1960, from London–Rome–Athens–Istanbul, London–Rome–Athens–Tel-Aviv and London–Moscow.

BEA successfully flew its Comet fleet – increased to 14 – on its longer routes; it was popular with passengers and returned a healthy profit for the airline. The aircraft were gradually replaced by the de Havilland Trident, and scheduled BEA Comet flights ceased in March 1969. They were stored at Cambridge, but a few were brought out to operate during peak periods in 1970 and 1971. It fell to G-APMA to fly the last scheduled BEA Comet service on 31 October 1971. However, with the formation of BEA Air Tours, Comets flew on, in modified BEA livery, until G-ARJL shut down on 31 October 1973, prior to being sold to Dan-Air. Olympic Airways purchased four Comet 4Bs in 1960 for operations in conjunction with BEA, linking the Mediterranean areas with London and the Middle East. These too ceased operating the type in March 1969; the aircraft were placed in open store at Marshall's Cambridge airfield.

Meanwhile, the Comet had been successfully demonstrated in South America and orders were forthcoming from Aerolíneas Argentinas for six Comet 4s – with the first passenger flight between Buenos Aires and Santiago on 16 April 1959 – and from Compagnia Mexicana de Aviacion (Mexicana) for the Comet 4C. This variant combined the wing of the Comet 4 with the fuselage of the 4B and was

BOAC inaugurated the first transatlantic crossing by fare-paying passengers on a jet airliner on 4 October 1958.

built for operations in hotter climates. Also attracted by this version were United Arab Airlines and Middle East Airlines, which subsequently ordered examples, as did King Ibn Saud of Saudi Arabia, who had one Comet 4C fitted out as a personal aircraft.

Aerolíneas Argentinas' services across the South Atlantic to Europe commenced on 19 May, and a Comet service from Buenos Aires to New York started soon afterwards. To cope with the demand for the three variants of the Comet, de Havilland were in full production at Hatfield and Chester.

EAA ordered two Comet 4s in 1958 for delivery in 1960. These two airliners – VP-KPJ and VP-KPK – were so successful on the Nairobi–London route that the airline ordered a third example (VP-KRL) for delivery in 1962. The aircraft continued to expand routes to Europe and to India as well as within Africa, and on occasion additional Comets were leased from BOAC and later from Dan-Air. EAA operated its last passenger Comet flight with 5Y-AMT (Dan-Air G-APDD) on 19 February 1971. Leased aircraft were returned and surplus airframes sold.

Mexicana received its first Comet 4C (XA-NAR) on 8 June 1960 and operated flights within Mexico as well as to the US. Passengers could travel in jet airliner style and speed to Los Angeles, Denver, Fort Worth, Dallas, San Antonio, Chicago and Miami from Mexico City. Mexicana's Comets differed in layout from standard examples with 22 first-class and 64 tourist class seats and, as always, proved popular, so much so that Mexicana considered taking up the option for two further aircraft, but instead decided to lease examples from BOAC when required. In turn, Mexicana leased two Comets to Guest Aerovia Mexico SA in 1961. Mexicana's option of two Comet 4Cs was taken over by Sudan Airways, which took delivery of the last Comet to be built at Hatfield. A company known as Westernair in New Mexico purchased the three Comet 4Cs from Mexicana with a view to operating them in an executive mode. However, this did not work out as planned, and two of the aircraft were subsequently scrapped with a third going to Boeing for its collection of aircraft at the Museum of Flight.

While the RAF were operating Comets during the Suez Crisis of 1956, Misrair of Egypt was in talks with de Havilland about buying Comets. The uncertain world of politics is clearly demonstrated here. With the formation of the United Arab Republic by Egypt and Syria, the airlines of the two countries were merged as United Arab Airlines (UAA).

In time, it ordered the Comet 4C, which was ideal for the climate and the routes flown by the airline. Nine examples were delivered and flew out of Cairo to Europe and also to Tokyo. These operated the Cairo–Bombay, Karachi, East and West Africa routes. Unlike the Mexicana examples, Egyptair (as UAA had been renamed) Comets had seating for 96 passengers in two classes. Unfortunately, five Egyptair Comet 4Cs were lost through accidents, mainly in adverse weather conditions, but the four remaining aircraft gave sterling service until they stood down in 1975. Before that, they had been taken off international routes and operated internal connections linking major towns. In 1976, they were sold to Dan-Air, which bought them for spare parts and broke the aircraft up in Cairo and at Lasham.

Aerolíneas Argentinas bought six Comet 4s and inaugurated it first Comet passenger flight between Buenos Aires and Santiago on 16 April 1959.

Seen outside the BOAC engineering base at London-Heathrow is Comet G-APDM. This aircraft operated the last scheduled BOAC Comet flight on 11 November 1965.

A smart new Comet 4B (G-APWA) in BEA livery photographed on its delivery flight to the airline.

Middle East Airlines (MEA) were based in the Lebanon and bought four Comet 4Cs; the first (OD-ADK) being delivered in December 1960, with scheduled services commencing on 6 January 1961. Known as Cedar Jets, they operated routes from Beirut to other Middle East destinations, as well as to Turkey, Greece, Austria, Germany, Switzerland, Italy and London. A typical Beirut–London flight took around 4½hrs, which was a vast improvement on the older piston-engined types. On 28 December 1968, MEA lost eight aircraft – three of which were Comets – when an Israeli commando group destroyed them, along with six other airliners belonging to different owners, in an attack on Beirut Airport. This was in retaliation for a Palestine Arab attack on an El Al Boeing 707 at Athens Airport two days earlier.

As a stopgap, MEA leased a Comet 4 and two Comet 4C from Kuwait Airways, along with other types from Ethiopian Airlines. The last MEA Comet 4C (OD-ADT) was withdrawn from service in November 1973 and sold to Dan-Air, which broke it up for spares at Lasham.

Comet 4C in the distinctive colour scheme of the Royal Aircraft Establishment.

Dan-Air made its last fare-paying Comet flight with G-BDIW on 9 November 1980.

Kuwait Airways Comet 4C seen at Beirut airport; its aircraft were later sold to Dan-Air in the UK.

Looking aft, we see the interior of a BOAC Comet 4, which had more comfortable seats than the piston-engined airliners of the day.

A night-shot of Malaysian Airways 9V-BAS, one of several ex-BOAC Comet 4s sold to the airline.

Sudan Airways and Kuwait Airways also bought Comet 4Cs from de Havilland; the former added two examples to its fleet in 1962 and operated them until 1975, when they were sold to Dan-Air. Kuwait Airlines ordered one Comet 4 and two Comet 4Cs, which were in operation between 1964 and 1966; they flew with the airline until offered for sale in 1968.

Across the Indian Ocean, Air Ceylon (later restructured as Air Lanka) chartered Comet 4 G-APDP from BOAC and commenced a weekly service to London and Singapore from Colombo airport in April 1962. The aircraft carried Air Ceylon titles and was joined by other leased BOAC Comet 4s during the 1960s; the airline operated six aircraft variously over the years until BOAC-leased VC-10s took over.

Unfortunately for the de Havilland aircraft, prospects in the UK for larger commercial transports were not forthcoming. There was no support from the government of the day; indeed, cancellations were more the order, and the next major blow came from Boeing with its massive 747. Boeing had experience with military aircraft, for which much government funding had been allocated, as well as commercial transports – its 707 was already a major influence on world air travel. BOAC, the airline that pioneered jet transport and kept faith with de Havilland, operated its last scheduled Comet flight with G-APDM from Auckland to London-Heathrow on 11 November 1965.

Chapter 7
End of the Line

Final days

Comets flew on with Dan-Air and a few other airlines, such as Channel Airways, which operated the ex-Olympic fleet and an ex-BEA Comet for a very short time on the inclusive holiday market in 1970. They also chartered other Comet 4s as required, but the enterprise was not successful, and the airline went into receivership in 1972. The last Comet passenger flight out of Heathrow was a Sudan Airways departure on 11 November 1972, 23 years after the prototype first flew. However, Comets were still to be seen at Gatwick, mainly in BEA and Dan-Air colours. The latter were to benefit from government cuts in 1975, which put paid to the last five Comet 4s (XR395–XR399) with 216 Squadron. These were sold to Dan-Air for commercial use as 4Cs with the civil registrations G-BDIT–BDIX, respectively.

Dan-Air was the last passenger operator of the de Havilland Comet in the UK and possibly anywhere else. It gradually withdrew the type as 1980 closed and made its last fare-paying flight with a group of enthusiasts from Gatwick on 9 November 1980, with Comet 4C G-BDIW. The airline was generous with the airframes, and several ex-Dan-Air Comets have survived; Duxford and Wroughton have examples, as do other collections in the UK and Europe, although some are only cockpit sections.

An independent de Havilland had been absorbed into the mighty Hawker Siddeley Aviation group, which also included Avro, and the latter had ideas about a replacement for the venerable Shackleton in the maritime reconnaissance (MR) role. The Comet airframe was ideally placed to be developed as the new-breed MR aircraft, which would be called the Nimrod.

Two civil Comet 4C airframes that remained unsold were selected for conversion as Nimrod prototypes XV147 and XV148 – the first fitted with Rolls-Royce Speys and flying from Chester on 23 May 1967, while the second, with Avons, flew from Woodford on 31 July 1967. Once again, John Cunningham was in charge of development flying. Ten years later, also from Woodford, Comet

Dan-Air Comet 4B G-APYD making a final landing before being donated to the Duxford Aviation Society for preservation.

Dan-Air Comet 4 G-APDB had flown with BOAC and other operators before coming to the charter airline. This aircraft is preserved in BOAC livery at Duxford airfield.

Channel Airways Comet 4B (G-APYC) flew with Olympic Airways and Dan-Air before being sold to the Ministry of Defence.

C4 G-APDS as XW626 took off on 28 June 1977 as the prototype Nimrod AEW 3. Later conversions were from Nimrods, but the project was cancelled when costs rose above acceptable limits. Comet/Nimrod XW626 was flown for the last time in August 1981 at RAE Bedford, where it languished for some years before being scrapped.

John Cunningham's name is inextricably linked with de Havilland products, in particular the Comet/Nimrod, and he retained great affection for both. He spoke about the latter to this author in 2001: 'Nimrod is in good service with the RAF as one of the most advanced maritime reconnaissance aircraft to date. To fly it is a great delight, not much different from the Comet 4C.' When Cunningham retired from British Aerospace, he stopped flying, except on two rare occasions: one was a flight on Lord Trefgarne's Devon and the other on Comet 4C XS235 before it was retired in late 1997. Being back on the flight deck held no surprises for Cunningham; he found it 'rather nice; it was all the same, very familiar. I was pleased they asked me'.

Another aspect that pleased John Cunningham at the time was the continued development of the trusted design, with the Nimrod airframes being adapted for the next generation Nimrod 2000 (later MRA4). This would have seen the recognisable Comet profile – although altered – flying well into the 21st century, some 60 years after G-ALVG first flew to herald a totally new form of civilian air transport. Sadly, we now know that this cannot happen, as Nimrod MRA4 was cancelled, and operational Nimrods were retired from service. That may be the end of the story, but the Comet lives on as the world's first jet transport airliner that blazed the trail for everything that followed, from Boeing 747s to Concorde and the Airbus 380. Not bad for a giant leap into the unknown prompted by a group of brave individuals planning a future for passenger air travel in the middle of a world war.

Comet 4 XW625, originally G-APDS with BOAC, was partially modified with a Nimrod fin and nose randome for the proposed Nimrod AEW 3.

Comet 4 flew with the RAE as XV814. Built in 1958 for BOAC (G-APDF), the aircraft was broken up in 1987.

Survivors

Several complete examples of the de Havilland Comet have survived in Britain and abroad.

Comet Survivors

Comet 1 G-ALYW
(Nose section) Lelystad, Netherlands

Comet 1A G-ANAV/CF-CUM
(Nose section) Wroughton, Wiltshire

Comet 1XB F-BGNX
(Fuselage) London Colney, Hertfordshire

Comet 1XB G-APAS
Cosford, Shropshire

Comet C.2 XK699
Old Sarum, Wiltshire

Comet C.2R G-AMXA/XK655
Sharjah, UAE

Comet 4 G-APDB
Duxford, Cambridgeshire

Comet 4 G-APDF – XV814
(Nose section) Privately owned, UK

Comet 4B G-APYD
Wroughton, Wiltshire

Comet 4C G-CPDA
Bruntingthorpe, Leicestershire

Comet 4C G-BEEX
Sunderland, Tyneside

Comet 4C G-BDIX
East Fortune, Scotland

The last flying example was Comet 4C XS235, which was operated from Boscombe Down until it was retired in March 1997. This aircraft is kept in ground-running condition at Bruntingthorpe.

Comet 4 G-APDB served with BOAC, MSA and with Dan-Air. Grounded, the aircraft was held at Lasham before being given to the Duxford Aiation Society. It has restored the aircraft and painted it in BOAC livery. (François Prins)

The ladies' powder room on BOAC Comet G-APDB has been superbly restored by the Duxford Aviation Society. (François Prins)

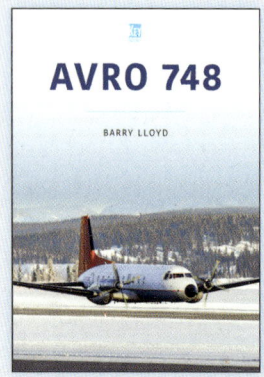
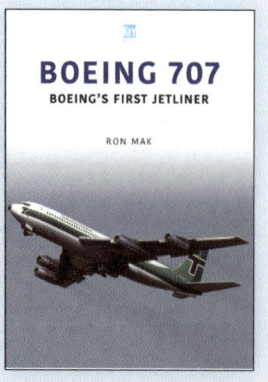
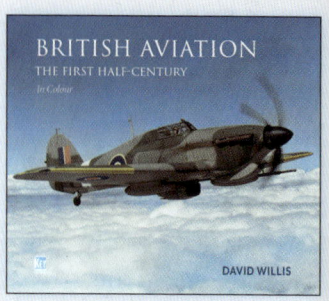

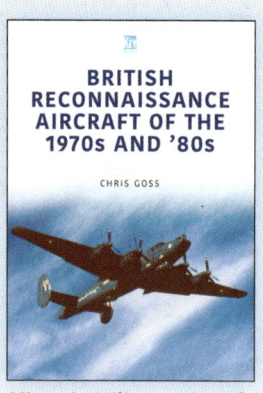